DISCARD

CONRAD SULZER REGIONAL LIBRARY
4455 N. LINCOLN AVE.
CHICAGO, ILLINOIS 60625

J097
G
525
V656
2003

SULZER

Dangerous crossings

S0-ACI-274

JUL   2004

The Restless Sea

DANGEROUS CROSSINGS

CAROLE GARBUNY VOGEL

Franklin Watts®

A Division of Scholastic Inc.
New York • Toronto • London • Auckland • Sydney
Mexico City • New Delhi • Hong Kong
Danbury, Connecticut

FOR JOYCE NETTLETON, a kindred spirit

ACKNOWLEDGMENTS

Many thanks to Professor Peter Guth of the Oceanography Department at the U.S. Naval Academy, who took time from his busy schedule to read and critique the manuscript and answer my many questions. His vast knowledge of the field and keen insight were reflected in his comments.

I am also grateful to Edward C. Monahan, Ph.D., D.Sc., the director of the Sea Grant College Program and a professor of marine science at the University of Connecticut at Avery Point, for sharing his immense scientific expertise.

I am indebted to Jeannine E. Talley, Associate Professor of English and Women and Gender Studies at the University of Guam, for sharing her incredible tale of survival in a capsized boat during a hurricane in the South Pacific.

Special thanks to fellow writer Dr. Joyce A. Nettleton for her invaluable criticism, insight, and sense of humor. I am thankful to students Stephen, Daniel, and Joanna Guth for reading the manuscript from the kid perspective.

I am most appreciative of editorial researcher Kathleen Derzipilski of San Diego, California, for a superb job of fact checking.

As usual, I am indebted to the reference librarians at Cary Memorial Library in Lexington, Massachusetts, for their assistance in tracking down hard-to-find information.

My sincere appreciation to my husband, Mark A. Vogel, for the encouragement and understanding that has become his hallmark. I would also like to acknowledge the many other people who helped either directly or indirectly.

Finally, my heartfelt thanks to my editor, Kate Nunn, for having faith in my writing ability and the talent to turn my manuscripts into spectacular books.

Photographs © 2003: Art Resource, NY/Scala: 50; Bridgeman Art Library International Ltd., London/New York: 1 (Christie's Images), 32 (Dixson Galleries, State Library of New South Wales), 35 (Ferens Art Gallery, Hull City Museums and Art Galleries, UK), 59 (The Argory, County Armagh, Northern Ireland); Corbis Images: 16, 17 (AFP), 8 (Craig Aurness), 30, 31, 66 (Bettman), 26 (Ralph A. Clevenger), 44, 45 (W. Perry Conway), 20, 21 (Aaron Horowitz), 28, 29 (Eric and David Hosking), 37, 42 (Hulton-Deutsch Collection), 40 (Peter Johnson), 10, 11 (Jose Luis Pelaez, Inc.), 14, 15, 22, 67, 69 (Reuters NewMedia Inc.), 38, 39 (Galen Rowell), 33 (Ron Sanford), 12, 13 (Stocktrek), 71 (James A. Sugar), 18, 19 (Sygma), 54 (Staffan Widstrand), 60; L.F. Tantillo: 48; Mother Courage Press/Barbara Lindquist: 4; Stone/Getty Images/John Lund: cover; The Art Archive/Picture Desk: 24, 25 (Ocean Memorabilia Collection), 52 (Dagli Orti/Naval Museum Genoa), 62, 65.

Book design by Marie O'Neill

Library of Congress Cataloging-in-Publication Data

Vogel, Carole Garbuny.
  Dangerous crossings / Carole G. Vogel.
  p. cm. — (The restless sea)
Summary: Relates stories of people who have faced terrible danger on or near the ocean and explains common causes of deadly conditions at sea, such as hurricanes, as well as other dangers, such as piracy and terrorism. Includes bibliographical references and index.
    ISBN 0-531-12325-1 (lib. bdg.)   0-531-16679-1 (pbk.)
    1. Shipwrecks—Juvenile literature. 2. Survival after airplane accidents, shipwrecks, etc.—Juvenile literature. [1. Shipwrecks. 2. Survival. 3. Ocean.] I. Title.
  G525.V556 2003
  910.4'52—dc21

2003005300

© 2003 Carole Garbuny Vogel
All rights reserved. Published simultaneously in Canada. Printed in the United States of America.
1 2 3 4 5 6 7 8 9 10 R 12 11 10 09 08 07 06 05 04 03

R0401491478

contents

CHAPTER 1
KILLER STORMS 5

CHAPTER 2
ICE AND DEATH 25

CHAPTER 3
SUNK BY A WHALE AND OTHER TERRIBLE MISFORTUNES 49

CHAPTER 4
PIRATES 61

GLOSSARY 73

FURTHER READING 75

SELECTED BIBLIOGRAPHY 77

INDEX 79

CONRAD SULZER REGIONAL LIBRARY
4455 N. LINCOLN AVE.
CHICAGO, ILLINOIS 60625

KILLER STORMS

For six years, two seasoned sailors Jeannine Talley and Joy Smith had sailed the South Pacific in *Banshee*, their 34-foot (10-meter) fiberglass boat. During that time they conquered many a nasty storm. But nothing had prepared them for the savage hurricane they chanced upon the night of June 6, 1990, 450 miles (700 kilometers) off the coast of Australia. As the storm strengthened, wave after wave pounded *Banshee*. The boat rocked violently. When it became unsafe to remain on deck, Jeannine and Joy retreated below to the main cabin. This room resembled the inside of an elegant house trailer.

With every large crashing wave, seawater seeped through the fastened ports and hatches. Everything in the forward compartment, a small room attached to the main cabin, became drenched. With growing fear, Jeannine and Joy wondered if *Banshee* could withstand such a brutal battering. Even their cat became jumpy.

The women decided to get some sleep. Joy worried that the fierce rocking would fling her to the floor. So she removed the foam pad from the upper berth where she normally slept and stretched out on the "cabin sole"—the floor. Amazingly, she fell asleep immediately. But Jeannine dozed fitfully in the lower bunk, the cat by her side.

As the hours passed, the storm continued to build. Sometimes the boat fell 15 to 20 feet (4.6 to 6 meters) into the steep troughs between waves, filling Jeannine with dread. She was better prepared than most people for hardship at sea. Before she had teamed up with Joy, she had run her own sailing school for women, called Seaworthy Women. But now her vast knowledge of the ocean came to haunt her. Jeannine knew that during this hurricane they might encounter a rogue wave—a gargantuan mountain of water towering above the other waves. A rogue wave could crack the boat in two.

This painting appeared on the cover of Jeannine Talley's book, *Banshee's Women Capsized in the Coral Sea.*

About five hours later, Jeannine's fears were realized when she heard the deafening roar of a rogue wave. Steep and cresting, the wave slammed the boat and pushed it dangerously to one side. Before the boat could right itself, a second mammoth wave struck. Crashing down on the deck, the wave submerged *Banshee* under tons of water. As the boat capsized, the sounds of shattering glass, flying cans, and the cracking of the mast filled the air. Jeannine was flung against the overhead of her bunk, and Joy slammed into a table. Miraculously, the boat righted itself and returned to the surface.

Though covered with hundreds of bits of broken glass from a shattered kerosene lamp, Jeannine was unhurt. Joy, however, was seriously injured. She had ruptured a major vein just below her knee, and it was bleeding internally. She was in terrible pain, and her leg was swelling.

The cabin was in chaos, yet a quick look around revealed no damage serious enough to sink the boat. Although *Banshee* was pitching wildly, both women went on deck to assess the breakage. Jeannine and Joy were terror-stricken by the sight. The sea was mountainous, with swells 50 feet (15 meters) high. Off to one side was the top of the broken mast, still firmly attached to the boat by wires. With each passing wave, the mast banged ominously against the boat. They realized that if *Banshee* rolled again, the mast could ram the boat with enough force to puncture it. But it was 2:00 A.M. and pitch-black. They would have to wait until daylight to cut the mast loose.

By daybreak, Joy's leg was swollen to twice its normal size and turning various shades of black, blue, and green. Joy took painkillers and laboriously crawled on deck. There, the women tackled the mast. Jeannine held it down while Joy sawed the thick wires with a hacksaw. They had to coordinate their efforts with the motion of the sea. Occasionally, savage squalls with wind speeds topping 100 nautical miles (1.8 kilometers) per hour forced them to retreat below deck. Winds that strong could have blown the women overboard despite the safety harnesses they wore to secure themselves to the boat. It took Joy and Jeannine more than three hours to release the mast.

Although the greatest danger had passed, the women remained in peril. The engine didn't work, the radio was broken, and Joy needed medical attention.

But they were confident that a search would be launched for them when they failed to make their scheduled 6:00 A.M. and 8:00 A.M. radio transmissions to their contacts ashore. Their boat's emergency beacon broadcast signals that could be picked up by ships, planes, and certain satellites.

A search plane spotted the women the afternoon of the first day, but oddly, no rescue boat followed. Four more days passed, and as they drifted, they grew more worried over Joy's leg. Her entire leg was now grossly swollen and had turned a deep shade of black.

Finally, on the fifth day a jet flying overhead saw them. Spotter planes soon followed. Within two hours, a large cargo ship pulled aside the battered *Banshee* and rescued the women and cat. Medical treatment saved Joy's leg. And the kindness of strangers saved the boat—two fishermen volunteered to bring it back. Jeannine and Joy spent the next 16 months repairing *Banshee* until it was sea-worthy again.

THE OCEAN AND ATMOSPHERE IN STEP WITH EACH OTHER

Stacked atop Earth's ocean is another ocean—an invisible one known as the atmosphere. The atmosphere rises more than 375 miles (600 kilometers) above the Earth. It does not have a distinct top like the ocean but peters out gradually.

The atmosphere wraps the planet's surface in a mix of many different gases, including mostly nitrogen, oxygen, and small amounts of argon, carbon dioxide, and water vapor (water in the form of a gas). Three-fourths of the gas mix is squeezed into the troposphere, the lowest layer of the atmosphere. Only 5 to 9 miles (8 to 14.5 kilometers) thick, the troposphere is where we live and where all weather begins and ends.

Both the ocean of water and the ocean of air move constantly. Powered by the Sun's energy and affected by Earth's gravity, their motions intertwine in an unending dance. Sunlight splashes on Earth's surface, heating the land and sea. The land and sea then warm the overriding air. The warm air expands and rises like a hot-air balloon into the atmosphere. Warm air is lighter and exerts less pressure than cold air does. Cooler, heavier air plummets down to replace it. At the surface of the sea, air moving horizontally churns up waves and propels currents.

Heat from the Sun is not spread evenly over Earth. Some areas of Earth's surface receive more solar energy than others. The Sun bathes the tropics—the wide belt on either side of the equator—with far more solar energy than the North and South Poles receive. As a result, the air above the tropics is significantly warmer and lighter than the air above the frigid poles.

Warm air creates lows—immense air masses of low pressure. Lows are the chief component of hurricanes, tornadoes, and blizzards. At the poles, cold heavier air forms highs—vast air masses of high pressure. When a huge cold air mass from the poles drifts toward the equator, it eventually bumps into a warm air mass moving out from the tropics. The meeting does not go tranquilly. Like warring armies, they clash along their fronts, often creating stormy weather. The cooler, heavier air pushes beneath the warm air mass and forces warm air upward. Earth's rotation causes the moving air masses to curve clockwise in the Northern Hemisphere and counterclockwise in the Southern Hemisphere. This creates high and low pressure systems that rotate in a circular path as they advance.

The greater the difference in air pressure between a high and a low, the faster the wind blows. If the difference is great enough and if other conditions in the atmosphere are right, a tornado or blizzard may develop.

Hurricanes: A Deadly Twist in the Partnership between Sky and Sea

Hurricanes brew over the sun-kissed waters near the equator in late summer and early fall. They do not depend on the presence of a high-pressure area to form. As the surface temperature of tropical oceans climbs to 79 degrees Fahrenheit (26 degrees Celsius) or higher, tremendous amounts of water evaporate, entering the atmosphere as water vapor. The warm, soggy air expands and rises skyward, forming a low pressure system. As the rising air expands, it also cools. The water vapor condenses, releasing heat, and changes back to liquid water in droplet form. Held aloft by the rising air, the drops collect into colossal clouds.

Eventually the massive clouds spawn clusters of violent thunderstorms. Sometimes the storms evolve into a larger storm called a tropical depression.

Most people give little thought to the boundary where air and water meet, including sailors who take advantage of the convergence.

9

In a tropical depression, the air at the ocean's surface spins in a circle around an area of low pressure. The winds in a tropical depression have a maximum speed of 38 miles (61 kilometers) per hour. Under the right conditions, a tropical depression becomes a tropical storm with rotating winds measuring 39 to 74 miles (63 to 119 kilometers) per hour. Some tropical storms mature into full-blown hurricanes with a wall of lightning-laced clouds that swirl around a column of low pressure. The low-pressure column—the eye of the storm—behaves somewhat like a chimney. It sucks in warm air from the bottom and funnels it upward like smoke. As the warm air streaks upward, more air streams in from all sides to replace it. The in-rushing air spins fiercely around the eye and enhances the fury of the spiraling clouds.

Within the clouds, winds rage, thunder roars, and rain pelts down. Yet the eye itself is a region of calm, often with a clear blue sky above it. The eye may extend from 5 to 40 miles (8 to 64 kilometers) across or even more. The strongest winds are closest to the eye, with a minimum speed of 74 miles (119 kilometers) per hour. The most ferocious hurricanes pack winds of up to 200 miles (320 kilometers) per hour. If you could harness all the energy released by a typical hurricane, it would provide enough electricity to power all

Palm trees whipped by hurricane winds

the homes and businesses in the United States for three or four years. Hurricanes can live for weeks fueled by the warmth of tropical waters. They fizzle out when they move over land or pass over cold water.

Hurricanes range from 300 to 1,000 miles (480 to 1,600 kilometers) in diameter. Wobbling like a spinning top, they weave across the water at a speed of 10 to 30 miles (16 to 48 kilometers) per hour. Their huge size and slow pace contribute to their destructive potential. Over land, hurricane winds can uproot trees and rip buildings from foundations. Torrents of rain may produce massive flooding. In the open ocean, hurricanes whip waves to tremendous heights, posing a deadly threat to even the largest ships.

As a hurricane approaches a coast, the winds drive waves 10 to 15 feet (3 to 4.5 meters) higher than normal. These waves claw away at fragile coastlines. At the eye, the low air pressure sucks up the sea's surface like a milkshake in a straw, creating a dome of water about 3 feet (1 meter) high. As the storm approaches the shore, the winds and the rising ocean floor lift the waves higher. The combination of the wind-driven waves and the dome from the low-pressure eye produces a storm surge—a rapidly rising wall of water at least 15 feet (4.5 meters) higher than the normal level of the ocean. The storm surge acts like a battering ram. If a storm surge coincides with a high tide, it is especially destructive.

This satellite image shows a powerful hurricane over Baja California. Note the well-defined eye in the center.

13

The Galveston Hurricane

The deadliest natural disaster in United States history took place in Galveston, Texas. Galveston was built on a large barrier island in the Gulf of Mexico. Although the island was 25 miles (40 kilometers) long and 2 miles (3 kilometers) wide, it protruded only 5 feet (1.5 meters) above sea level in most areas. In September 1900, a monster hurricane slammed the island, which was home to 38,000 people. The buildings in Galveston had been constructed to survive storm flooding. The first floors were placed about 3 feet (1 meter) above ground level. But they were not raised high enough for this storm. The hurricane pushed the seas much higher than normal, submerging low-lying areas in 10 feet (3 meters) of water and higher ground in 4 to 5 feet (1.2 to 1.5 meters). When the storm surge struck on top of this flood, it contributed immensely to the 6,000 to 8,000 lives lost.

In 1998, Hurricane Mitch struck Central America, killing at least 11,000 people, primarily in Honduras and Nicaragua. Most destruction and loss of life resulted from mudslides and flooding in mountainous regions. So much rain fell during a short period of time that the soil could not soak it up and rivers could not contain it. The clear-cutting of rain forests for timber and the slash-and-burn farming used to free up forested land for agriculture contributed to the disaster. In the preceding years, these

A street in Galveston, Texas, after a catastrophic hurricane in 1900 devastated the city

14

practices had destroyed half of Honduras's tree cover and nearly 60 percent of Nicaragua's, leaving hillsides barren. With no tree roots to anchor the soil, and little plant life to slow runoff, water cascaded over fields and mountainsides. It turned the ground to soup and triggered thousands of mudslides. Floods and slides swept away entire villages and their inhabitants.

Mitch was the deadliest hurricane to strike the Atlantic Ocean since the Great Hurricane of 1780, which snuffed out the lives of about 22,000 people on three Caribbean islands. Hurricanes occur more frequently in the western Pacific Ocean, where they are referred to as typhoons and cyclones. In 1970, when a cyclone hammered the subcontinent of India, high winds combined with a storm surge left half a million people dead in low-lying Bangladesh.

This humongous landslide triggered by rainfall from Hurricane Mitch buried five villages in Nicaragua and killed some 11,000 people.

Floodwaters from Hurricane Mitch inundated fishing villages along the Honduran coast, such as this one in La Mosquitia.

The Perfect Storm

In October 1991, three weather systems, including a late-season hurricane, combined into "The Perfect Storm"—a perfectly deadly one, that is. The first system started as a low over the Great Lakes. It blew east, straddling the Canadian border, and then swept across Maine and Nova Scotia, strengthening along the way. Eventually it collided with a high swinging down from the icy Arctic. The two vastly different air masses clashed over the North Atlantic. They created a nor'easter—a mighty tempest with violent winds and heavy rains blasting from the northeast off the coast.

The nor'easter was a monster in its own right. But when Hurricane Grace swirled up the eastern seaboard from the Caribbean and fused with it, the hurricane turned into a powerful maelstrom. One meteorologist likened the event to throwing gasoline on a raging fire. The Perfect Storm was a hurricane 2,000 miles (3,200 kilometers) wide, stretching over the Atlantic from Jamaica to Labrador, Canada. Its winds barreled over the ocean and reached sustained speeds of more than 80 miles (130 kilometers) per hour.

The longer and faster a wind blows, and the bigger an area it covers, the taller and steeper the waves it generates. As the Perfect Storm peaked off the coast of New England, the ocean waves became murderous mountains. Some towered more than 100 feet (30 meters) high—the height of a 10-story building. Twelve people perished in the storm, including the six-man crew of the *Andrea Gail*, a fishing boat from Gloucester, Massachusetts. The tragic fate of the fishermen was immortalized in the book *The Perfect Storm* by Sebastian Junger and in a movie of the same title.

This is an artist's conception of the *Andrea Gail* confronting a boat-swallowing wave during the Perfect Storm.

18

TORNADOES AND WATERSPOUTS

The weather pattern over the central United States during late spring and early summer often breeds tornadoes. The stage is set when a warm, moist air mass flowing north from the Gulf of Mexico smashes into a cold, dry air mass traveling south from Canada. The cold air swoops beneath the warm air, jolting it upward. The volatile mix produces a squall—a narrow line of thunderstorms.

In 1 percent of squalls the air rushing in begins to rotate around a small area of low pressure. Like a hurricane, the winds nearest the middle whirl the quickest, with speeds ranging from 40 to 250 miles (65 to 400 kilometers) per hour or more. A funnel forms from the spinning air and drops down from the thundercloud. The air in the funnel swirls upward. If the funnel touches the ground, it sucks up dirt and practically anything else in its path.

The United States holds the record for the greatest number of tornadoes annually—about 1,000. Most occur in "Tornado Alley," a wide swath of land extending from Texas and Oklahoma through Kansas and Nebraska. Usually tornadoes last for only a few minutes, but exceedingly destructive ones may rage for hours. In 1925, the Tri-State Tornado took the lives of 689 people in a 3 1/2–hour rampage across portions of Missouri, Illinois, and Indiana.

A tornadic waterspout is a tornado that occurs over water. It sucks up water instead of dirt and can be just as lethal as those that move over land. In 1970, a tornadic waterspout along the coast of Italy capsized a yacht and scoured a campground, killing a total of 47 people and injuring hundreds of others.

A building remains untouched as a tornado wreaks havoc in a neighboring cornfield.

Fair-weather waterspouts form tornado-like funnels over a lake or ocean and are often mistaken for tornadoes. They can develop in fair weather under puffy cumulous clouds when spinning air rises over a body of warm water. Fair-weather spouts are actually tornadoes in reverse—funnels that climb up from the sea to the sky.

Waterspouts suck up water in their funnel to a height of 20 feet (6 meters). The rest of the moisture in the funnel consists of freshwater droplets condensed from the air. Sometimes spouts vacuum up fish and other marine life with the water. More common than storm-generated spouts, fair-weather spouts are typically smaller and less dangerous. The skies over the Florida Keys produce 400 to 500 waterspouts a year, more than any other place in the world.

This tornadic waterspout over the Mediterranean Sea caused extensive damage in the coastal town of Limassol, Cyprus, on January 27, 2003. Thirty people were injured.

chapter 2

ICE AND DEATH

More than 80 years ago, the world was stunned by the sinking of the *Titanic*, the grandest ocean liner of its time. Deemed unsinkable, the *Titanic* set sail on April 10, 1912, on its first voyage, a transatlantic crossing from Southampton, England, to New York City. On the fifth night out, the *Titanic* grazed an iceberg and sank, taking with it 1,513 lives. Although other ships in the area had broadcast warnings about icebergs, the *Titanic* was traveling close to full speed when the collision occurred. Compounding the catastrophe was a shortage of lifeboats. Only 705 people survived.

The International Ice Patrol was established in 1914 in response to the loss of the *Titanic*. During iceberg season—typically from February to July—the ice patrol tracks icebergs in the North Atlantic and tells mariners how to avoid them. Since its inception, the ice patrol has not lost a single ship in its territory to an iceberg.

Most icebergs that threaten shipping break off from the ice sheet that covers four-fifths of Greenland, the world's largest island. The ice sheets blanketing the continent of Antarctica produce bigger icebergs than Greenland's, but they rarely drift into shipping lanes.

A watercolor painting of the *Titanic* sinking

The ice sheets of Greenland and Antarctica cover about 10 percent of Earth's land surface, with an average thickness of 7,000 feet (2,100 meters). Antarctica's ice sheets shroud an area twice the size of Australia. They took at least 25 million years to develop. Much younger, Greenland's ice sheet is one-tenth the size of Antarctica's. The ice sheets in both places originated from snow that never melted. In these polar landscapes, the temperature never climbed high enough to melt all the snow that piled up. Year after year, new snow accumulated atop the old.

Fresh snow looks white and fluffy because air is trapped between the crystals of frozen water. Gradually, the tremendous weight of the overlying layers of snow compresses the lower layers, squeezing out the air. The frozen water fuses into larger and larger ice crystals. The color of the ice changes from white to brilliant blue as the snow loses air and becomes solid ice.

Ice sheets serve as vast storehouses of freshwater, locking up 75 percent of the world's supply. If the ice sheets in Antarctica and Greenland melted completely, they would release enough water to raise the global sea level more than 200 feet (60 meters).

Ice sheets flow out in all directions. Tugged by gravity, the ice moves toward the sea. Where an ice sheet juts out far past the shoreline, it forms floating ice shelves. The world's largest ice shelf is Antarctica's Ross Ice Shelf, which extends 450 miles (700 kilometers) over the Antarctic Ocean. It is roughly 600 miles (950 kilometers) wide and 1,000 feet (300 meters) thick.

In Greenland, coastal mountains prevent the ice sheet from reaching the ocean in all but a few areas. Where the ice sheet does meet the sea, it does so in narrow channels called glacier tongues. Large blocks of ice frequently split away from glacier tongues and ice shelves. The blocks float off as icebergs.

Perhaps the largest iceberg in living memory is "Godzilla," a 1,000-foot (300-meter) thick slab of ice nearly the size of Connecticut. Godzilla snapped off Antarctica's Ross Ice Shelf in the year 2000.

This is a composite photograph, consisting of four different images. It shows how an iceberg would appear if you could see all of it at once.

The Sinking of the *Britannic*

The *Titanic*'s younger but slightly larger sibling, the *Britannic*, also met a tragic end. Under construction at the time of the *Titanic*'s demise, the *Britannic* was subjected to extensive safety improvements. A second skin was constructed inside its hull and the watertight bulkheads were extended. These design features would have saved the *Titanic*. Unfortunately, they could not help the *Britannic*. The British government had requisitioned the *Britannic* for use as a hospital ship during World War I. The ship's lavish interior was converted into operating rooms, intensive care units, and hospital wards. Along with two other converted luxury liners, the *Britannic* ferried soldiers wounded on the mainland of Europe back to England. Filled to capacity, the *Britannic* could transport 3,300 injured troops.

In 1916, on its sixth voyage, the ship apparently struck a mine—a bomb placed in the water by an enemy vessel. The mine exploded and tore a hole in the hull near the bow. The ship began to list and the first six watertight compartments flooded. The *Britannic* could have withstood this damage. However, in preparation for the arrival of wounded soldiers later in the day, the nurses had opened most of the ship's windows to air out the rooms. The flooded forward compartments caused the ship to settle low enough in the sea for water to pour through the openings. Had the windows been closed, the *Britannic* could have survived and limped back to port for repairs.

Instead, the ship sank in less than one hour. Enough lifeboats were available for all the 1,066 people aboard. But the still moving propellers sucked

Only the top one-tenth of an iceberg peaks above the waterline. The rest lies hidden beneath the waves.

29

in two of the lifeboats, resulting in the deaths of about 30 people. If the ship had been filled to capacity with injured soldiers, the death toll might have rivaled the *Titanic*'s.

THE GREAT ARCTIC ICE DISASTER OF 1871

Icebergs are not the only hazard to ships in frigid waters. Pack ice—frozen seawater—can develop rapidly in polar seas and crush a hapless vessel. In the late 1800s, a miscalculation of pack ice behavior dealt a devastating blow to the Yankee whaling industry.

Yankee whaling started shortly after the Pilgrims established the Massachusetts Bay Colony in 1620. At first the settlers only harvested dead or stranded whales along the coastline. Then the colonists began to hunt whales offshore. They stripped the dead whales of blubber—the thick blanket of fat beneath the skin—and boiled it to obtain whale oil. Before the discovery of petroleum and natural gas and the invention of electricity, burning whale oil in lamps provided the best lighting.

Within a century, whales became scarce along the New England coast. Enterprising Yankees built large wooden sailing ships called whalers, which could roam far from land in pursuit of their prey. The whalers carried smaller catcher boats—long rowboats sometimes outfitted with a single sail—to use in the actual chase. The whalemen targeted sperm whales, right whales, and other species that moved slowly enough to be harpooned and floated when dead. In time, so many of these whales were slaughtered that they became difficult to locate. A profit could no longer be made hunting them in the Atlantic. So the Yankee whalemen sailed around the tip of South America to pursue whale herds in the Pacific and Indian Oceans.

Far more ships have been lost to torpedoes and mines than icebergs. The *Britannic*—shown here at her launching—sank off the coast of Greece after striking a mine.

The flames on the decks of these whaling ships are deliberate. They come from tryworks—brick furnaces used to boil strips of blubber to extract whale oil.

Yankee Whaling

Whaling was to early Americans what ExxonMobile and the rest of the oil industry is to present-day Americans. Whales were regarded as living oil deposits waiting to be tapped. Whaling ships were outfitted for long voyages in the bustling seaports of Nantucket and New Bedford, Massachusetts. These towns also provided a marketplace for the sale of the whale oil upon a ship's return.

In 1859, oil was discovered in Pennsylvania. This event launched the petroleum industry and reduced the demand for whale oil. Yankee whaling declined in the decades that followed. But the demand for baleen prevented it from dying out entirely. Baleen whales, such as blue whales, humpbacks, right whales, and bowheads, have baleen plates instead of teeth. Long and thin, baleen plates consist of the same stiff but flexible material as human fingernails. The plates hang down from a whale's upper jaw like teeth on a comb. Meshed together they act like a filter and enable the whale to strain food from water. Craftspeople turned baleen into watch springs, buggy whips, umbrella ribs, and whalebone corsets.

This photo shows two feeding humpback whales.

The desire for baleen took whalers to the Arctic Ocean along the northern coast of Alaska, where bowheads lived in abundance. Hunting in these waters was risky business. From autumn to late spring the Arctic Ocean freezes over and is covered by one gigantic ice pack. During summer, the pack typically breaks up into floes—floating masses of ice in all shapes and sizes. This fragmented, frozen landscape drifts constantly. Colliding floes may fuse together while individual floes may be wrenched apart. Bowheads congregate in the water between the melting ice pack and land. Like right and sperm whales, bowheads swim slowly and do not sink when dead. The trick for the whale hunters was to kill the bowheads and retrieve their carcasses without being crushed by the shifting floes.

During the summer of 1871, the hunt went well, even though the ice pack was breaking up more slowly than usual. On August 29, the wind shifted and pushed the ice pack toward shore, wedging 33 whaling ships in a narrow channel of open water. The whalemen waited for the wind to shift and free them. But the channel continued to fill with ice and on the tenth day the remaining open spaces began to ice over.

Salt as Antifreeze

The salt in seawater slows the development of ice crystals. Instead of freezing at 32 degrees Fahrenheit (0 degrees Celsius) like freshwater does, seawater turns to ice at approximately 29 degrees Fahrenheit (-2 degrees Celsius), depending on the amount of salt. As seawater solidifies, the salt cannot fit inside the ice crystals so it is pushed out. The leftover salt increases the salinity of the surrounding water. Because this cold, saltier water is more dense than typical seawater, it sinks and may join a deep-ocean current flowing sluggishly along the seabed.

Oceans freeze in the same manner as ponds and lakes—from the top down. At first, ice crystals cloud the water, forming a layer of slush. Long slicks of thin ice congeal on the surface, like grease scum on cooling soup. The "grease ice" thickens into a thin sheet of ice. Waves and wind break the sheet into "pancake ice"— round pieces with upturned edges. Jostled by the motions of air and water, the pancakes jam together to form ice floes.

Whalemen from Hull, England, hunted right whales in the Arctic waters near Greenland. This oil painting from 1822 depicts several whalers in Arctic waters, including one trapped in ice.

34

Unfortunately for the whalemen, this freezing process had transformed the channel into an ice sheet over 1 foot (30 centimeters) thick. More than 1,200 people were stranded. Most were whalemen, but some of the captains' wives and children were also onboard. By September 9, the ice floes had crushed three ships. Wintering on the northern coast was not an option. The ships carried provisions for three months, and winter in this barren region lasted closer to nine.

In an act of desperation, the captains dispatched a small crew in three catcher boats to search for the seven whaling ships in the fleet that had remained outside of the ice. On September 12, the crew returned. They had discovered a narrow passage through the ice and had found the seven whalers, which lay about 70 miles (110 kilometers) away. Incredibly, all the stranded people made it to safety using the catcher boats.

The next summer a crew returned to the Arctic to recover any ships that may have survived the winter. Only one vessel was salvageable. Five years later, 13 whaling ships were lost to Arctic ice, and another 5 were destroyed in 1888. The American whaling industry never fully recovered from these disasters.

Whaling in Other Nations

Although American involvement in whaling decreased after the Arctic ice disasters, whale hunting by other countries escalated. Norwegian and other European whalemen replaced sail-powered boats with steam-powered ships and motorized catcher boats. They improved the tools for killing and processing. Whale species that had previously eluded slaughter because they swam fast and sank when dead were no longer safe. As a result, the majestic blue, sei, and fin whales became easy targets.

New markets for whale products opened. Using the process of hydrogenation, liquid whale oil was changed into a solid fat. This, in turn, was used to manufacture margarine, soap, and cosmetics. Whale oil was even used as auto transmission fluid. Electric freezers permitted the storage of whale meat. The Japanese, with little land suitable for raising cattle, relished this beeflike food source. As modern whaling thrived, most whale populations were decimated. Right, blue, and fin whales were hunted almost to extinction.

This photograph from 1905 shows whales that have been slaughtered by Norwegian whalemen and will be towed to a factory along the coast of Spitsbergen, Norway, to be butchered.

After World War II, the International Whaling Commission (IWC) was established to regulate the hunting of whales. Since 1986, the commission has banned its members from participating in commercial whaling, and some species are beginning to recover. However, IWC member nations Japan and Norway are defying the ban and continue to hunt whales. Iceland, which is not an IWC member, also hunts whales.

NORTH POLE VERSUS SOUTH POLE

Despite similarities in their harsh, bitter-cold climates, the regions at the top and bottom of the world are a study in contrasts. The North Pole is crowned by a permanent layer of sea ice overlying the Arctic Ocean. The South Pole is located on the rocky, ice-clad continent of Antarctica.

Most of the Arctic Ocean is ringed by land, like a gigantic lake. In winter it freezes over completely. By the end of the winter, the first-year ice has a thickness of 5 to 6 feet (1.5 to 2 meters). More than half the Arctic ice pack survives the summer and increases in thickness the following winter. With little room to spread out, floes slam into each other, creating immense ridges up to 70 feet (20 meters) high. Arctic ice floes last

These ice floes near the North Pole range in thickness from 28 to 47 inches (71 to 120 cm). Unlike icebergs, which form from freshwater (snow), ice floes form mainly from salty seawater.

39

between 3 and 10 years. Some eventually drift south into the North Atlantic and melt.

The Antarctic Ocean surrounds Antarctica and provides plenty of room for pack ice to spread out. Wrapped around the continent, the Antarctic pack ice stretches more than 60 miles (100 kilometers) out to sea by the end of each winter. The ice rarely grows more than 3 feet (1 meter) thick, and much of it melts in the summer. Melting pack ice does not raise the level of the sea because it floats and has already displaced its equivalent mass in water.

Both Arctic and Antarctic waters are home to fish, seals, birds, and whales. Polar bears are the best known Arctic creatures, while penguins are the most famous residents of the Antarctic.

Sir Ernest Shackleton and the *Endurance*

One of the greatest survival tales of all time is that of the Trans-Continental Expedition to Antarctica. In 1912, Irish explorer Sir Ernest Shackleton decided to lead the first trek across the frozen Antarctic wilderness. His plan was to sail into the Weddell Sea, a southern arm of the Atlantic Ocean, to the coast of Antarctica. He and his men would then cross the South Pole using dogsleds and wind up at the Ross Sea on the opposite side of the continent. There, a second ship would be waiting for them. It took Shackleton more than a year to organize his expedition. In December 1914, he and his crew of 27 sailors and scientists sailed into the ice-choked Weddell Sea on their ship the *Endurance*. Unbeknownst to Shackleton, the weather was unusually cold and the pack ice extended farther north than normal. The expedition would never set foot on Antarctica.

About 100 miles (160 kilometers) from land, ice ensnared the ship. For more than half a year, the *Endurance* was frozen fast in ice, drifting northwest away from Antarctica. In August 1915, the ice shifted. In slow motion, it began to crush the immobilized vessel. By October, the ship's wooden hull could no longer withstand the pressure. The timbers cracked and water poured in, forcing the men to move onto the pack ice. Within a month, the ship disappeared beneath the sea.

In summer, icebergs sheer off from the edge of the ice sheet covering Antarctica. In winter, they may become trapped by sea ice. Most icebergs melt within two years or so.

41

For five months, the marooned men camped on the ice, hunting penguins and seals and fighting boredom and cold. In April 1916, the ice broke up, allowing Shackleton to launch three lifeboats salvaged from the *Endurance*. Powered by sails and oars, the boats wove through giant icebergs and stormy seas to desolate Elephant Island, 100 miles (160 kilometers) away. The treacherous journey took a week with daily rations consisting of one hot drink and a hardtack biscuit. Nearly 500 days had passed since the adventurers had last felt solid ground beneath their feet.

Unfortunately, the closest outpost—a whaling station—was on the island of South Georgia, 800 miles (1,300 kilometers) to the northeast. Leaving most of the men behind, Shackleton and a crew of five headed for South Georgia in the sturdiest lifeboat. Hungry, cold, and thirsty, the men battled raging winds and 50-foot (15-meter) waves. They had only a sextant, binoculars, a compass, and a few navigation charts to help them find a small speck of land in an immense ocean. Despite the dismal odds, they reached South Georgia 16 days later. But they had landed on the wrong side.

So Shackleton and two of the men trekked 17 miles (27 kilometers) across a rugged, ice-studded mountain range to reach the whaling station. Their disheveled appearance—more than a year had passed since they had last bathed, shaved, or cut their hair—frightened two boys they met at the edge of the outpost. Once inside the whaling station, the men were given hot food, a warm bath, and clean clothes. Their comrades on the far side of South Georgia were soon picked up. Pack ice, however, delayed the rescue of the men on Elephant Island by four months. Despite the cold and other hardships not a single life was lost on the expedition. Afterward, the expedition's members identified Shackleton's outstanding leadership ability and his sensitivity to their needs as the key to their survival.

A Threat to Polar Bears

Polar bears are more creatures of the sea than of land. They use pack ice as a platform to stalk ringed seals—their favorite prey—and other animals. Polar bears have a sense of smell a hundred times more sensitive than humans'. They can sniff out baby seals hidden in tiny caves that the mother seals dug in the ice.

This is an actual photograph of the *Endurance* trapped in Antarctic ice. Despite the extreme cold and primitive living conditions, photographer Frank Hurley succeeded in making a stunning photo documentary of the trials faced by Shackleton and his men.

Polar bears also hunt seals by waiting motionless next to breaks in the ice. When a seal surfaces to breathe, the bear bites its head and hauls the animal onto the ice. There it is finished off. Occasionally, polar bears feast on other types of seals, seabirds, young beluga whales, or baby walruses.

Polar bears must store up enough fat to carry them through the summer months when their hunting grounds disappear. When the ice melts, the bears move onto land. They eat little or no food until the ice re-forms in the fall. Global warming—the gradual rise in world temperature—may spell doom for the bears by extending the ice-free period. The bears' hunting season in Canada's Hudson Bay has already been shortened by at least three weeks since 1980. There, sea ice has begun to melt earlier each spring and freeze later in fall. The local bears are skinnier than before and more cubs are dying of starvation. According to some climate scientists, the entire Arctic Ocean may be ice-free in summer by 2080. This would result in mass starvation of polar bears and their eventual extinction.

Global warming also poses a threat to penguins in Antarctica. Krill, which are the penguins' major source of food, eat the algae that grow on the bottom of sea ice. If global warming causes less sea ice to form, there will be less algae. Less algae means fewer krill in

A mother polar bear must gain more than 400 pounds (180 kg) in one summer to sustain herself and her cubs during pregnancy and nursing. Typically she gains it all in about four months and then fasts for eight months, six of which she spends in an ice cave.

45

Antarctica, and ultimately fewer penguins and other animals such as whales and seals, which also depend on krill.

Global Warming

Global warming is the gradual increase in the average world temperature. During the twentieth century, the average global temperature rose about 1.1 degrees Fahrenheit (0.6 degrees Celsius). The temperature rise was not evenly distributed across the globe—some places had a greater temperature rise than others. Certain tropical seas became hot enough to kill coral reefs. Glaciers capping mountains far from the poles have melted significantly, and the permafrost (permanently frozen soil) in Alaska, Northern Canada, and other northerly regions has begun to thaw.

Rising temperatures will evaporate more water from the ocean, fueling larger hurricanes, tornadoes, and blizzards. In addition, the patterns of rainfall and temperature will shift, changing weather. Dry climates may become rainier. Rainier climates may experience long droughts.

During the twentieth century, global warming caused the sea level to rise 4 to 10 inches (10 to 25 centimeters). Over the next 100 years, the sea level could climb another 4 to 35 inches (9 to 88 centimeters), depending on how quickly Earth's atmosphere warms. At the same time, the average global temperature will probably increase 2.2 to 10 degrees Fahrenheit (1.4 to 5.8 degrees Celsius). The extra heat will shrink glaciers and ice caps, releasing enough water for the sea level rise. Much of the water will come from the ice sheet over Greenland. Some animals, including polar bears, penguins, and coral, will not be able to adapt fast enough to survive the environmental changes brought by global warming.

People living in coastal areas worldwide will also be severely affected. Particularly vulnerable are those who make their homes in the Maldives, the Marshall Islands, and other low-lying islands that poke no more than 10 feet (3 meters) above sea level. Equally at risk are people who live in unprotected river deltas, such as those found in Bangladesh, Vietnam, China, Egypt, and along the Louisiana coast in the United States.

Climate experts attribute the rise in global temperature to human activity, mainly the burning of oil, coal, and gas. The combustion of these fossil fuels releases carbon dioxide into the air. Carbon dioxide is one of the so-called greenhouse gases that help regulate Earth's temperature. (The other major greenhouse gas is water vapor.) Greenhouse gases absorb some of the infrared energy—or heat—given off by Earth. This warms the gases, which in turn warm the surrounding air. The gases also radiate some of the infrared energy back to the planet's surface. Carbon dioxide occurs naturally in the atmosphere, but the burning of fossil fuels has significantly increased the amount of carbon dioxide in the air.

chapter 3

SUNK BY A WHALE AND OTHER TERRIBLE MISFORTUNES

In August 1819, the whaler *Essex* set sail from Nantucket Island, Massachusetts, with Captain George Pollard at the helm. The ship carried a crew of 21 men, 7 of whom were African Americans. Like the white crewmen aboard any whaling ship, the black men on the *Essex* were paid according to their rank, not their race. (This was quite remarkable, since at that time slavery was permitted in the United States.) All the men on a whaler received a percentage of the profits at the end of the voyage. For the average crewman, this did not amount to much.

On the *Essex*, the black whalemen slept in separate quarters from the white whalemen, but both groups received the same poor quality of food. They subsisted on hardtack (dried-out biscuits, the consistency of plaster) and meager portions of salt pork or beef (meat preserved in heavily salted water). The three white officers, however, ate freshly baked bread and plenty of vegetables while the supply lasted. Thirty hogs raised on the ship provided the officers with an ample supply of fresh meat.

The *Essex* was heading to the South Pacific to hunt sperm whales. Initially, the whaling got off to a dismal start. Barely any prey were found. But by the end of the first year, the hunting had improved and the ship had half its quota of whale oil. Low on provisions, Captain Pollard stopped along the coast of Ecuador to pick up drinking water and fresh fruit and vegetables. One of the crew, a black man fed up with life aboard the *Essex*, took the opportunity to desert. This brazen act probably saved his life.

The captain next sailed to the Galápagos Islands to stock up on sea turtles, about 300z in all. The average turtle weighed about 80 pounds (35 kilograms). Stacked like cordwood, the turtles could survive more than a year in the ship's

An artist's rendition of the *Essex* leaving Nantucket

hold without food or water. When slaughtered, the turtles still provided moist, tasty meat.

Harvesting sea turtles in vast numbers was standard practice for mariners in those times. The men gave no thought to the harm inflicted on turtle populations. They considered turtles, like whales, to be theirs for the taking.

With enough food and water to last for months, the *Essex* hoisted sail for the whaling grounds near the equator. On November 20, 1820, the whalemen found themselves near a large herd of sperm whales about 1,500 miles (2,400 kilometers) west of the Galápagos. Soon the chase began. The whalemen launched their three small catcher boats, six men to a craft, leaving two crewmen onboard the *Essex*. Captain Pollard took charge of the first catcher boat, First Mate Owen Chase, the second, and Second Mate Matthew Joy, the third. In short order each group targeted its prey.

In a typical kill, the crew rowed alongside a whale and the man in the front of the boat hurled a harpoon into it. The harpoon was attached to a long rope, which was secured to the boat. When the injured whale tried to flee, it dragged the boat along at breakneck speeds. After several miles the whale tired, and the hunters moved in to finish the job.

For Pollard and Joy, the kills went as expected. But the whale harpooned by Owen Chase flicked its tail against the boat, ripping the side open. To keep from sinking, the men jammed their coats and shirts into the hole. Then they raced back to the *Essex* to make repairs.

While First Mate Chase patched the catcher boat, a male sperm whale, 85 feet (26 meters) in length, approached the *Essex*. It was the largest sperm whale the men had ever seen, but they did not sense danger. The whale appeared to study the ship and then, unexpectedly, charged it. The animal slammed the hull with so much force that it knocked the crewmen off their feet.

The whale floated quietly next to the ship while it recovered from the blow. Then it swam a short distance away and began to snap its jaws and slap the water with its tail. Working itself into a frenzy, the whale attacked the *Essex* once more. This time it dealt the ship a mortal blow, punching a large hole in the hull. As the vessel filled with water, the whale swam away, never to return.

This Currier & Ives lithograph shows whale hunters in their small catcher boats going in for the kill.

51

The men scrambled to collect equipment and provisions. In the 10 minutes before the *Essex* capsized, they saved two navigation books, two sets of navigation equipment, and two of the officers' trunks. Meanwhile, the crews of the other two catcher boats watched in horror as the *Essex* disappeared. Immediately, they cut loose their whales and rejoined their shipmates. They found the *Essex* on its side, low in the water. It was still possible to salvage more necessities, including 600 pounds (270 kilograms) of hardtack, 200 gallons (760 liters) of water, firearms and ammunition, boat nails, and six turtles. The captain distributed everything equally among the three catcher boats, except for the navigation materials. He kept one set of navigation equipment for himself and gave the other to First Mate Chase. Second Mate Joy was left at a severe disadvantage. If he lost contact with the other boats, he would be unable to find his way.

For the next two days, the catcher boats hovered near the wreck. Using planks from the stricken ship, the crew raised the sides of each catcher boat by about 6 inches (15 centimeters), for added protection against storm waves. They also cut the sails from the *Essex* and sewed them into smaller sails for the catcher boats. Then each craft was fitted with two masts and a jib, turning them into sailboats.

The men were now as ready as they would ever be. The nearest land, the Marquesas Islands, lay 1,200 miles (1,900 kilometers) away, but the men had heard rumors (later proved to be wrong) that the natives were cannibals. Concern about unfriendly natives caused them to dismiss the Society Islands, about 2,000 miles (3,200 kilometers) to the southwest, as a destination, too. So they decided to head for South America, nearly 2,500 miles (4,000 kilometers) to the east. However, the prevailing winds and current were against them in their present location. If they first sailed due south for 1,500 miles (2,400 kilometers), they would have an easier time heading east toward South America. They calculated that the roughly 3,500-mile (5,600-kilometer) voyage would take 56 days. So they rationed the food to last two months. Each man received 2 cups (0.5 liters) of water daily along with 6 ounces (0.2 kilograms) of hardtack, equal in calories to six slices of bread.

Thirst quickly became a constant torment. Within days, it was joined by the ravages of hunger. On November 30, the men on each boat sacrificed a turtle. First they drank the blood, and then they cooked the meat inside the shell.

In the foreground of this picture, whalemen struggle to right their small catcher boat after a whale has overturned it. The focus of the art, however, is the large whaling ship and the dead whale next to it. The whale is being On deck, the blubber will be cut into small pieces and boiled.

A Galápagos turtle

The feast invigorated the men and raised their spirits, but only temporarily. Starvation quickly returned. On December 10, they devoured the remaining turtles.

By December 14, it became necessary to cut the hardtack rations in half. Desperately hungry, the men scraped barnacles off the bottom of their boats and ate the shrimplike organisms inside. Fishing was not an option. The part of the ocean they were crossing was barren, like a desert.

On December 20, the crew landed on an uninhabited island. The only freshwater source was a spring that was covered by seawater except at low tide. Nevertheless, this early Christmas present was sufficient to rehydrate the men. They stayed on the island for a week, subsisting on fish, birds, and eggs. The castaways almost depleted the island's wildlife. Even so, when the time came to move on, one man from each boat decided to stay behind and take his chances on the island.

The rest of the men departed with their casks of water full and some fish and birds for sustenance. Within days, starvation came to haunt them again and the men feared for their lives. By January 10, Second Mate Joy became the first to die. His shipmates sewed him in his clothes and tied a stone to his feet before burying him at sea.

Shortly afterward, a storm separated Chase's boat from the others. They never caught up with each other again. With food running low, Chase cut the hardtack rations on his boat by half and then by half again. One of his crewmen died of starvation. Like Matthew Joy, he was buried at sea.

Around the same time, starvation stole another life on Joy's boat. This time, however, the men on Joy's and Pollard's boats made the difficult decision to eat their dead shipmate. A few days later, another man died, and his body too was used to prolong the lives of the others. Within a few days, the grisly scene was repeated twice more.

On January 29, the crew on Captain Pollard's boat lost track of Joy's boat, which still held three men. These three were never heard from again. By February 6, the four remaining men on Pollard's boat hovered close to death. They decided to cast lots to decide who would sacrifice himself for the sake of the others. Owen Coffin, the captain's 18-year-old cousin, lost. He was killed by gunshot. Five days later, another man succumbed to starvation, and his remains sustained the other two.

On Owen Chase's boat, one of the four men died. The survivors wrestled overnight with the repugnant choice of resorting to cannibalism. In the morning, they reluctantly ate their shipmate. On February 18, close to their destination on the South American coast, Chase and his two companions were picked up by an English ship. Eighty-nine days had passed since the *Essex* had sunk. Five days later, another ship rescued Pollard and his companion. The three men who voluntarily marooned themselves on an island were also saved.

The three white officers had been the best nourished of all the men aboard the *Essex*, and two of them survived. The fat reserves in their bodies probably gave them an advantage. Six other white members of the crew lived. But all six black crewmen died, even though rations had been distributed equally throughout the ordeal. Since both the white and black crew members endured the same inferior diet prior to the sinking of the *Essex*, perhaps ethnic differences explain the disparity in the death rates. It has been suggested that American blacks tend to have less body fat than whites of the same height. This would put blacks at a disadvantage to survive starvation conditions.

Fire on the Circus Ship

One of the most bizarre sea tragedies occurred in October 1836, when the steamship *Royal Tar* burst into flames with a circus aboard. The circus, known as Dexter's Locomotive Museum and Burgess' Collection of Serpents and Birds, was en route from Saint John, New Brunswick, to Portland, Maine. It had just finished a successful season touring Canada's easternmost provinces. Among the many animals in its menagerie were one tiger, two camels, two pelicans, one antelope, six horses, at least one lion, and an elephant named Mogul. A brass band rounded out the troupe. Such an impressive enterprise required much equipment, including large circus wagons for transportation and a big treasure chest laden with silver and gold coins—the season's handsome profits. Unfortunately, to fit the entire circus on the ship, two of the *Royal Tar*'s four lifeboats had to be removed.

A few days out of Saint John, strong winds along Maine's coast forced the vessel to seek shelter in Penobscot Bay. While anchored, the ship's engineer emptied the water from the boilers to make some repairs. Boilers are crucial to the operation of the paddle wheels on a steamship. To power the wheels, wood or coal is burned in a furnace. The heat from the burning fuel changes the water in the boilers from a liquid into steam. The steam expands and drives the engines that turn the paddle wheels.

When the engineer completed his repairs, he gave the order to refill the boilers. But the order was ignored. When the furnaces were fired up, the boilers became blistering hot and ignited the ship. Flames raced through the vessel, panicking both the humans and the caged animals.

The two remaining lifeboats could not hold the 93 people clamoring to escape. Amid the commotion, 20 of the stranded men tried without luck to push a large wooden circus wagon overboard to use as a float. An effort to build a raft proved more successful. The raft was launched over the side and quickly loaded with a small group of men. Just as the men pulled away from the ill-fated ship, the elephant broke free from its restraints. Trumpeting in terror, the beast crashed through the ship's railing. It landed directly on the raft and killed all the men.

The elephant resurfaced a few minutes later and tried to swim to land, 5 miles (8 kilometers) away. Days later, its lifeless body drifted near one of the islands dotting the rocky coastline. The horses faired somewhat better. Released into the water, three managed to reach shore. The other three swam frantically around the flaming ship until they tired and drowned. Trapped in their cages, the rest of the animals died in the blaze.

Meanwhile, the captain of the *Royal Tar* took command of a small ship that had come to the rescue. He managed to save dozens of people. In the end, only 32 human lives were lost. The casualties included women and children because the tradition of saving them first had not yet been established.

ORIGIN OF THE CRY "WOMEN AND CHILDREN FIRST"

The HMS *Birkenhead* was a steamboat built for the Royal Navy in 1845, at the peak of the British Empire. This was the era when the British ruled about one-quarter of the people of the world and claimed one-fifth of the land. Occasionally, populations under British rule rebelled, and Great Britain would send in its military to squelch the uprisings. One place experiencing unrest was South Africa, where Xhosa tribesmen struggled for control of their own lands.

In early 1852, the *Birkenhead* transported reinforcements from the British Isles to South Africa, a 47-day journey. Two giant paddle wheels propelled the vessel, but the ship also had a tall mast and was fully rigged for sailing. On February 25, after taking on supplies at Simonstown on the southern tip of Africa, the ship headed for a military outpost just a two-day voyage away. Most of the 638 persons aboard were soldiers and sailors. However, there were 7 women and 13 children—family members of some of the military personnel. There were also 30 horses—the mounts of army officers.

At two the next morning, the *Birkenhead* struck a hidden rock along the treacherous South African coast. The rock gouged a large hole in the hull. Water immediately flooded the engine room. It then poured into the neighboring compartment where 150 soldiers were sleeping in hammocks. Only a few soldiers managed to escape. They emerged half-dressed and joined the other sleep-dazed, panicked survivors on deck. Despite the desperate situation, the soldiers and sailors awaited their orders.

Hoping to pull safely away from the rock, the ship's captain gave the command to reverse the engines. The paddle wheels whirred and the ship lurched backward, tearing the gash wider. Now the ship took on water faster. The horses, wild with fear, threatened the safe evacuation of the lifeboats. So the captain instructed the men to move the animals over the gangway and into the sea, assuming that the horses would instinctively swim the few miles to shore. Then he gave the order to save the women and children first. There were anguished farewells as some of the wives had to be torn away from their husbands.

The *Birkenhead* carried only eight lifeboats. Tragically, only three could be successfully launched. As the *Birkenhead* sank lower and began to tilt, the soldiers not assigned to lifeboats stood motionless on the slanting deck. Silently they awaited their fate.

Moments before the doomed ship plummeted to the depths, the captain issued an ill-conceived order. He urged all those able to swim to try to reach the lifeboats. Immediately, two other officers rescinded the command. They realized that if the men clambered onto the lifeboats, the boats would be swamped and everybody would drown. They commanded the men to stand fast.

Amazingly, the men obeyed. Only when the sea washed over them did the troops break ranks and try to save themselves. About 50 men clung to the top of the ship's mast, which poked some 30 feet (9 meters) above the waves. Others grasped floating wreckage. Some swam toward shore, only to drown in the heavy surf. Still others made it safely to the beach, where one astonished officer found his horse waiting for him. In the morning, a passing schooner picked up the survivors in the water, including those in the lifeboats. Exact figures for the casualties are unknown. However, some records show that 445 people died and 193 survived, including all the women and children.

The demise of the *Birkenhead* established the maritime tradition of saving women and children first. This practice still endures more than 150 years later.

A Modern Sea Tragedy

In August 2000, the *Kursk*, a nuclear-powered Russian submarine, was participating in routine military exercises in the Barents Sea off of Russia's northern coast. Suddenly, an explosion ripped through the sub. A second blast followed a couple

The men aboard the HMS *Birkenhead* had been sleeping at the time of the collision and were either in nightshirts or completely naked. They didn't have a chance to dress before the ship sank. So this illustration of the *Birkenhead* tragedy is not historically accurate because most of the men are shown in dress uniform.

58

minutes later. Experts think that a torpedo developed a leak and accidentally exploded. The resulting fire set off the other torpedoes near it. The damaged submarine plunged to the bottom of the sea. Most of the 118 crewmen aboard died quickly, but 23 survived and huddled together in the rear compartment. Although the submarine lay in water only 350 feet (100 meters) or so deep, the pressure was too great for the men to try to swim to the surface. A rescue effort could not be launched in time.

More than two months later, divers retrieved 12 bodies from the wreckage, including that of 27-year-old Dmitri Kolesnikov. Tucked in Kolesnikov's pocket was a letter wrapped in plastic. The letter, addressed to his wife of only a few months, described the accident and the aftermath. Kolesnikov wrote that the survivors knew they were doomed. Investigators speculate that the men may have suffered in the cold and the dark for as long as three days before dying.

The submarine was eventually recovered and taken to port, where most of the remaining bodies were retrieved.

PIRATES

The most powerful pirate in history was not a handsome, bold, swashbuckling, man. She was Cheng I Sao, a ruthless Chinese woman, who with her husband built up a fleet of nearly 2,000 ships. With a crew of 50,000 thugs she and her husband attacked cargo vessels in the South China Sea and terrorized fishing villages along the shore. Cheng I Sao and her followers showed no respect for human life. When raiding villages they sometimes slaughtered every man, woman, and child. At other times they took prisoners, holding them for ransom or forcing them to join the crew. Prisoners who tried to escape were executed or tortured. One common torture technique was to nail the victim's feet to the deck of the pirate ship.

Cheng I Sao married into piracy in 1801. Her husband, Cheng I, controlled a pirate fleet, which was organized into six squadrons. Traditionally, the wives of Chinese pirates lived, worked, and raised their children aboard pirate ships. They fought side by side with their husbands in battle. Cheng I Sao fought so skillfully that Cheng I rewarded her with her own squadron. In 1807, Cheng I died. Cheng I Sao took command of the entire fleet and expanded it.

She ran her pirate empire like a business. One of the main sources of profit was extortion. Cheng I Sao demanded protection money from ships and coastal settlements in exchange for not attacking them. She was savvy enough to recognize that she needed the support of some communities to ensure a steady flow of food for her followers. So she made arrangements with the farmers of certain villages to buy their rice, grapes, and other crops. She guaranteed a reliable supply of gunpowder in the same way. As part of her agreement with helpful villages, she promised to behead any pirate who harmed them.

Cheng I Sao adopted a strict code of conduct for her pirates which had three basic rules:

Chinese pirates attacking a trading ship

1. If a man went ashore without permission, his ears were punctured as punishment. If he did it a second time, he was put to death.
2. All plundered goods were registered and placed in the fleet's warehouse. A pirate was entitled to one-fifth of anything he stole. Pilfering from the warehouse was punishable by death.
3. No man could use a female captive for his own pleasure without permission from the ship's purser (treasurer). Using violence against any woman or marrying a woman without her consent was punishable by death.

The pirates lived in squalor on the ship. Each man was allocated only 4 square feet (0.4 square meters) of living space. Most of the men were unmarried. Those who had wives shared their tiny space with their families. The filthy quarters swarmed with rats, insects, and other vermin. Occasionally these pests provided a nutritional boost when eaten with rice or in soup. The pirates subsisted mainly on fish and rice. Their best meals were the result of ransoming captives for pigs or chickens. In their free time, the pirates smoked opium and gambled in card games.

The Chinese Imperial Navy tried to defeat Cheng I Sao's fleet, but failed. Finally, in 1810, the emperor of China decided to buy off the pirates. One by one the commanders of Cheng I Sao's squadrons accepted pardons and lucrative government posts. Then they used the vessels under their command to help the imperial forces hunt their former associates. Discouraged, Cheng I Sao decided to quit piracy, too. In return for her allegiance, the emperor gave her and her second husband amnesty. The husband also received a military appointment. But Cheng I Sao could not entirely abandon her life of crime. In her later years, she ran an infamous gambling house.

PIRATES AND PRIVATEERS

Piracy has existed since ancient times. At least 4,000 years ago, rogue sailors realized they could make a living by raiding ships, extorting ransoms, harassing coastal settlements, and enslaving people. While many pirates were greedy outlaws with no respect for human life, others were so impoverished that they turned to piracy out of desperation. Some pirates were captured seafarers, forced to choose between death or turning pirate. Shipments of gold and silver were the

This pirate squadron is under attack. Note that these pirate ships are *junks*—large flat-bottomed wooden sailing vessels with square fronts.

63

prized booty. But seagoing bandits stole everything they could sell or use themselves, including sugar, candles, tools, pots, and rolls of cloth. Plundered barrels of rum never went to waste in pirate ships.

Some nations sponsored piracy. They gave private shipowners letters of marque—a license to rob the merchant ships of enemy nations. These legal pirates—dubbed privateers—brought their spoils back to port and auctioned it off. The government took a portion of the proceeds, and the owner and crew split the rest.

Blackbeard, the most diabolical pirate in American history, started as a privateer. He was one of thousands of pirates who terrorized the shipping lanes of the Americas during the Golden Age of Piracy, from the mid-1600s to 1725.

According to legend, Blackbeard was a giant of a man, who stood 6 feet 4 inches tall (193 centimeters). He wore a bright red jacket and sported a sword and an assortment of daggers in a holster at his waist. Across his chest he strapped bandoliers stuffed with two or three pistols.

Blackbeard's real name is usually given as Edward Teach. His nickname came from his immense coal-colored beard, which covered his face almost entirely. The beard started just below the eyes and extended halfway down his chest. Blackbeard braided his wiry facial growth into long dreadlocks and twisted them around his ears. His aim was to look as formidable as possible. For a finishing touch, he tucked pieces of slow-burning rope beneath his wide-brimmed hat. He ignited them just before going into battle. A living nightmare, Blackbeard correctly calculated that the fiercer he looked, the more likely his victims would be to surrender without a fight.

It is reputed that, in a drunken rage, Blackbeard shot one of his cronies in the knee and crippled him for life. When asked why, Blackbeard supposedly replied that if he did not kill one of them now and then, they would forget who he was.

Blackbeard is said to have married at least 12 times. He took a new wife in every port without divorcing the previous one. It is reported that he liked to see his wives dance. He would sit back in a comfortable chair and order his wife to perform. To make her steps more lively when she slowed, he held a pistol in each hand and peppered her steps with carefully aimed shots. He barely missed the toes. This continued until the poor women collapsed from exhaustion.

A portrait of Blackbeard as imagined by an artist

Blackbeard took command of his own ship in 1717. He worked up and down the coast of the Carolinas, seizing any ship he desired. He murdered any crew that resisted and sank their ships. The secluded, shallow coves and bays along North Carolina's Outer Banks provided secure hideouts for him. At his peak, Blackbeard led four ships and a crew of at least 300 men. This force seems paltry compared with Cheng I Sao's fleet. But it was sufficient to strike fear in the hearts of his unlucky victims.

Blackbeard paid kickbacks to Governor Charles Eden of the North Carolina Colony. When merchants, sea captains, and plantation owners appealed to Eden to clamp down on Blackbeard, their pleas went unheeded. Finally, they turned to Governor Alexander Spotswood of the Virginia Colony. Spotswood, who hated piracy, agreed to help. But he knew that the Royal Navy's warships were too heavy to pursue Blackbeard in the shallow waters where the pirate hid. Using his own funds, Spotswood hired two small sloops that could negotiate the shallows.

B. Cole sculp.

Blackbeard the Pirate.

Blackbeard's final battle

The Royal Navy used the sloops to defeat Blackbeard in one short but extremely bloody battle in late 1718. The pirate's head was severed and tied to the bow of one of the vessels. Blackbeard was among the last of the infamous pirates in the Atlantic. The Golden Age of Piracy ended when Britain and the colonial governments recognized that safe trade routes served their business interests better than piracy. After that, naval warships patrolled the coastlines, hunting down the rogues. Pirate ships could not match the tremendous firepower of a warship. While some pirates such as Blackbeard died in spectacular battles, others were captured and hung. Many ordinary pirates accepted amnesty and became peaceful citizens.

Modern Marauders

Piracy has never completely disappeared. After a lull of nearly 300 years, it is on the rise again. There were 469 reported pirate attacks in the year 2000, resulting in the deaths of 72 people. Today, robbery on the high seas flourishes in the shipping lanes off Asia, Africa, and South America. Plagued by poverty and political upheaval, these regions lack effective law enforcement.

As in the past, greed and the lure of easy money motivate modern-day pirates. But instead of sailing in wooden ships with the Sun and stars for guidance, the new breed of sea robbers relies on powerful speedboats equipped with the latest navigation equipment and communications gear. Their weapons have evolved from

To combat piracy, the Indonesian navy monitors all ships through its busiest shipping lanes. These "suspects" are participants in a navy drill to demonstrate how the antipiracy task force works.

cannons, cutlasses, and pistols into a high-tech arsenal of automatic rifles, rocket-propelled grenade launchers, and antitank missiles. The treasures they seek are now cameras, computers, watches—any cargo of value—along with the vessels themselves.

Contemporary pirates target merchant ships and tankers. Typically, these vessels sail with small, unarmed crews. They make easy pickings for raiders, who simply empty the ship's safe and steal the crew's valuables. In more sophisticated heists, crooked port workers supply sea thugs with computerized inventories showing exactly where the most valuable freight is stowed. Crime syndicates protect and control much of the piracy in Asia. They bribe corrupt law enforcement officials to look the other way.

Occasionally, pirates kill a ship's crew and seize the vessel. Repainted, renamed, and provided with false documents, the hijacked ship can then be sold for an immense profit on the black market. These disguised vessels may be used in smuggling people, including young Asian women, who are sold into slavery of the worst sort.

In 1998, Chinese and Indonesian pirates swarmed aboard the freighter *Cheung Son*. The pirates massacred the entire crew of 23, heaved the bodies overboard, and stole the vessel. However, they did not get away with their dastardly deed. While investigating another crime, Chinese police supposedly stumbled across photographs of the pirates partying on the *Cheung Son*. The authorities arrested the band. Thirteen of the pirates received death sentences and 19 others were given prison terms. The ship was never found.

VIETNAMESE BOAT PEOPLE AND THAI PIRATES

In the years after the Vietnam War ended in 1975, at least 900,000 Vietnamese found life under Communist rule so intolerable that they risked their lives for freedom. They fled Vietnam by boat, crowding into small crafts never intended for ocean use.

Professional pirates, as well as Thai fishermen turned pirate, preyed on these refugees. They beat the boat people and stole their valuables, even going so far as to rip gold teeth from their mouths. (In some countries dentists commonly use

gold to repair cavities.) The pirates were extremely savage. They brutally assaulted many of the women and girls and sometimes abducted them. They murdered the men and boys who tried to protect the women. Almost half the Vietnamese boats that reached foreign lands had been terrorized at least once by seagoing gangs. No one knows how many Vietnamese boat people died on the high seas. Estimates range from 50,000 to 100,000 or more men, women, and children. It is widely believed that pirates were responsible for most of the deaths, while starvation and drowning also took a significant toll.

Brazilian "Water Rats"

In 2001, Brazilian pirates, known as "water rats," killed Sir Peter Blake, a world champion yachtsman. Blake had twice led the New Zealand sailboat team to victory in the prestigious America's Cup race.

Blake had been interested in the impact of pollution on underwater ecosystems, and he had just completed a three-month research expedition up the Amazon River. His schooner was anchored near the mouth of the Amazon when a small group of pirates raided it. Blake ran for his rifle and shot one of the intruders in the hand. Another bandit returned fire. He shot Blake twice in the back, killing him. The murderer was caught but claimed self-defense.

PIRACY AS A TOOL OF TERRORISM

Modern-day terrorists use piracy for political purposes. In 1985, four heavily armed Palestinian terrorists hijacked the Italian luxury liner *Achille Lauro* off the coast of Egypt. About 400 people were onboard. The hijackers demanded the freedom of 50 Palestinian prisoners held in Israeli jails. To show they meant business, the terrorists shot and killed a wheelchair-bound American passenger, 69-year-old Leon Klinghoffer. They then threw his body and wheelchair overboard. The Egyptian government, unaware of the cold-blooded murder, negotiated the surrender of the terrorists. The Egyptians agreed to give the terrorists safe passage in exchange for the release of the ship and its passengers. When the U.S. government learned of Leon Klinghoffer's execution, it sent navy F-14 fighters to intercept the

Egyptian jet carrying the hijackers to freedom. The jet was forced to land in Sicily, and the terrorists were taken into custody by Italian officials.

SAFER SEAS

Political will and military action can reduce the threat of terrorism on the high seas. But the natural forces that have always made the ocean a dangerous environment will always remain. These include strong winds, hurricanes, storm waves, rogue waves, icebergs, sea ice, and poor visibility. Advances in technology

A U.S. Coast Guard vessel splashes through heavy seas during training exercises.

have made ocean travel much safer for ships. Satellites and other weather forecasting equipment help predict storms, menacing winds, and high seas. Radar warns ships of approaching vessels, so collisions can be averted. High-tech communications equipment allows the crews of stranded or shipwrecked vessels to call or signal for help. In the territorial waters of the United States, the highly skilled U.S. Coast Guard is trained to rescue crews of downed boats, even in the most treacherous seas. Icebreakers—ships equipped to break through ice—can keep shipping lanes clear and rescue unfortunate boats locked in ice. Future advances in technology will make the seas even safer.

Glossary

Algae—simple plantlike organisms containing chlorophyll but lacking roots, stems, and leaves

Amnesty—the granting of freedom to a criminal; a pardon

Atmosphere—the mixture of gases that surrounds Earth

Baleen plate—a row of stiff hornlike material that hangs down from the upper jaw of a baleen whale

Barnacle—a small shrimplike crustacean that attaches itself to a rock or the water-covered surface of a boat and forms a hard shell

Barrier island—a ridge of sand that rises above the ocean surface offshore but does not connect to land

Cannibal—a human who eats the flesh of another human

Cargo—freight; the goods or merchandise transported by ship

Catcher boat—a large rowboat used to hunt whales

Current—a broad band of water that flows through the ocean

Cutlass—a short, curving sword

Equator—an imaginary line drawn around the center of Earth halfway between the North and South Poles

Global warming—the gradual increase in the average world temperature caused by the burning of oil, gas, and coal

Hardtack—dry, hard biscuits

High—a region of high air pressure

HMS—an abbreviation for His Majesty's ship or Her Majesty's ship

Hull—the frame of a ship

Hurricane—a severe tropical storm that begins at sea and has winds of at least 74 miles (119 kilometers) per hour

Hydrogenation—the process by which a liquid oil is combined with hydrogen and changed into a solid fat

ICE FLOE—a mass of floating ice in the sea that formed when seawater froze

ICE SHEET—an immense mass of ice originating on land from compacted snow

ICEBERG—a mass of floating ice in the sea that originated as part of an ice sheet or glacier on land and broke away

KRILL—tiny shrimplike animals

LIFEBOAT—a relatively small boat carried on a large ship that is used to evacuate people during an emergency

LOW—a region of low air pressure

NOR'EASTER—a powerful rainstorm or snowstorm with strong northeast winds blowing in from the Atlantic Ocean toward the coast of Canada or New England

PACK ICE—frozen seawater

PARDON—amnesty

PIRATE—a criminal who commits robbery, torture, or murder on the high seas

PREY—animals that are eaten by other animals; humans that are victimized by other humans

PRIVATEER—a sailor on a ship licensed to attack the ships of enemy nations

SEA LEVEL—the height of the ocean

SHIPPING—ships that carry cargo

SHIPPING LANE—a common route for ships traveling from one port to another

SPECIES—a distinct kind of plant, animal, or other organism

TERRORISTS—people who use violence or the threat of violence in an attempt to achieve their goals

TORNADO—a violent, rapidly spinning, funnel-shaped cloud that touches down from a thundercloud and moves over a narrow path on land

TROPICAL DEPRESSION—a tropical storm over the ocean with winds of no more than 38 miles (61 kilometers) per hour

WATERSPOUT—a tornado-like funnel that forms in relatively calm weather over water

WHALEMEN—sailors who hunt whales

WHALER—a large sailing ship designed for long whale-hunting voyages

WHALING—the hunting of whales

YANKEE—someone from New England or the northeastern United States

Further Reading

BOOKS

Ballard, Robert D. *Ghost Liners: Exploring the World's Greatest Lost Ships*. Boston: Little, Brown, 1998.

De Pauw, Linda Grant. *Seafaring Women*. Boston: Houghton Mifflin, 1982.

Kimmel, Elizabeth Cody. *Ice Story: Shackleton's Lost Expedition*. New York: Clarion, 1999.

Lauber, Patricia. *Hurricanes: Earth's Mightiest Storms*. New York: Scholastic, 1996.

Meltzer, Milton. *Piracy & Plunder: A Murderous Business*. New York: Dutton Children's Books, 2001.

Steele, Philip. *Pirates*. New York: Kingfisher, 1997.

Vogel, Carole G. *Nature's Fury: Eyewitness Reports of Natural Disasters*. New York: Scholastic Reference, 2000.

MAGAZINE ARTICLES

Eliot, John L. "Polar Bears: Stalkers of the High Arctic." *National Geographic*, January 1998, pp. 52–71.

WEB SITES

"The Actual 'Perfect Storm': A perfectly dreadful combination of nature's forces," by Beth Nissen
CNN nature Web site

http://www.cnn.com/2000/NATURE/06/30/perfect.storm/

"The Cryosphere: where the world is frozen," a Web page hosted by the National Snow and Ice Data Center.

http://nsidc.org/cryosphere/

"The Shrinking Polar Bears," CBC Web site

http://www.tv.cbc.ca/national/pgminfo/warming/bears.html

"Terror on the Waves: Pirates still exist—and they're just as ruthless as ever," by Andrew Chang, ABC News Web site

http://abcnews.go.com/sections/world/DailyNews/piracy010129.html

"Understanding Waterspouts," USA Today Web site.

http://www.usatoday.com/weather/tornado/wtspouts.htm

"Warnings from the Ice," a Web page hosted by NOVA, deals with the question of what would happen to the world's coastlines if Antarctica's ice sheets melted

http://www.pbs.org/wgbh/nova/warnings/waterworld/

"Whaling," Greenpeace; be sure to click on "The animated story of whaling"

http://whales.greenpeace.org/whaling/index.html

"You Wouldn't Want to Be a Polar Explorer," a Web site that summarizes Ernest Shackleton's voyage.
http://www.salariya.com/web_books/explorer/

Selected Bibliography

BOOKS

Barnes-Svarney, Patricia, and Thomas E. Svarney. *Skies of Fury: Weather Weirdness around the World*. New York: Simon & Schuster, 1999.

Duxbury, Alyn C., Alison B. Duxbury, and Keith A. Sverdrup. *An Introduction to the World's Oceans*. 6th edition. New York: McGraw-Hill, 2000.

Earle, Sylvia A. *Sea Change: A Message of the Oceans*. New York: G.P. Putnam's, 1995.

Junger, Sebastian. *The Perfect Storm: A True Story of Men against the Sea*. New York: Norton, 1997.

Kerr, J. Lennox. *The Unfortunate Ship: The Story of H.M. Troopship Birkenhead*. London: George G. Harrap & Co., 1960.

Philbrick, Nathaniel. *In the Heart of the Sea: The Tragedy of the Whaleship* Essex. New York: Viking, 2000.

Snow, Edward Rowe. *True Tales of Pirates and Their Gold*. New York: Dodd, Mead, 1953.

____. *True Tales of Terrible Shipwrecks*. New York: Dodd, Mead, 1963.

Talley, Jeannine. *Banshee's Women Capsized in the Coral Sea*. Racine, WI: Mother Courage Press, 1992.

PAMPHLETS, MAGAZINE AND NEWSPAPER ARTICLES

Brooke, James. "Whalers and Their Foes Enlist Scientists," *New York Times*, June 4, 2002, Section F, page 1.

Cerquone, Joseph. *Uncertain Harbors: The Plight of Vietnamese Boat People.* Washington, D.C.: U.S. Committee for Refugees, October 1987.

_____. *Vietnamese Boat People: Pirates' Vulnerable Prey.* Washington, D.C.: U.S. Committee for Refugees, February 1984.

WEB SITES

"The Antartic [*sic*] pack-ice ecosystem," by Jane E. Stevens, *Bioscience* online. volume 45, number 3, (March 1995)

"Chapter 4: Flight from Indochina" in *The State of the World's Refugees 2000: Fifty Years of Humanitarian Action,* by Mark Cutts, et al. United Nations High Commissioner for Refugees. Also published in book form by Oxford University Press.

http://www.unhcr.ch/pubs/sowr2000/ch04.pdf

"Ice shelves float on the sea," USA Today Cold Science: Reports on the Antarctic and Arctic

http://usatoday.com/weather/resources/coldscience/aiceshlf.htm

"Mitch: The Deadliest Atlantic Hurricane Since 1780," NOAA National Climatic Data Center Web site

http://www.ncdc.noaa.gov/oa/reports/mitch/mitch.html

"Polar Ice." NASA Facts: The Earth Science Enterprise Series, April 1998

http://eospso.gsfc.nasa.gov/ftp_docs/Polar_Ice.pdf

"Waterspouts" by Bruce B. Smith, a meteorologist with the National Weather Service

http://www.crh.noaa.gov/apx/science/spouts/waterspouts.htm

Index

Achille Lauro, 70
African Americans, 49, 55
Alaska, 34
algae, 45, 73
amnesty, 63, 73
Antarctic Ocean, 41
Antarctica, 27, 41, 46
Arctic Ocean, 34, 39, 45
atmosphere, 7–9, 46–47, 73

baleen plate, 33, 73
baleen, 33–34
Barents Sea, 58
barnacle, 54, 73
barrier islands, 14, 73
Birkenhead, 57–58, *59*
Blackbeard, 64–66
Blake, Peter, 70
bowhead, 34
Britannic, 29, *30*, 31

cannibal, 53, 55, 73
cargo, 7, 61, 73
catcher boat, 36, *52*, 53, 73
Chase, Owen, 51, 53, 55
Cheng I Sao, 61, 63
Cheng Son, 68
Coffin, Owen, 55
coral reefs, 46
current, 53, 73
cutlass, 68, 73
cyclone, 16

Dexter's Locomotive Museum and
    Burgess' Collection of Serpents
    and Birds, 56

Eden, Charles, 65
Elephant Island, 43
Endurance, 41, *42*, 43
equator, 9, 73

Essex, *48*, 49, 51, 53, 55
eye of the storm, 11

fossil fuels, 47
funnel, 21–22

Galápagos Islands, 49, 51
Galveston, Texas, 14, *15*
glacier tongues, 27
glaciers, 46
global warming, 45–47, 73
grease ice, 34
greenhouse gases, 46
Greenland, 25, 27

*H*MS, 57, 73
hardtack, 49, 53, 54, 73
high, 9, 73
high tide, 13
Hudson Bay, 45
hull, 29, 41, 73
Hurricane Mitch, 14–16
hurricane, 9–19, 46, 71, 73
hydrogenation, 36, 73

ice floe, 34, 36, *38*, 39, 73
ice pack, 34, 39
ice sheet, 25, 27, 36, 73
ice shelves, 27
iceberg, 4, 25, *26*, *40*, 71, 74
International Ice Patrol, 25
International Whaling Commission
    (IWC), 39

Joy, Matthew, 51, 53–54
Junger, Sebastian, 18
junks, *62*

Klinghoffer, Leon, 70
Kolesnikov, Dmitri, 59
krill, 45–46, 74

Kursk, 58

letters of marque, 64
lifeboat, 25, 29, 43, 56, 58, 74
low, 9, 74
low-pressure column, 11

Malacca Straits, *67*
Maldives, 46
maritime tradition, 58
Marquesas Islands, 53
Marshall Islands, 46

Nantucket Island, 49
nor'easter, 18, 74
North Pole, 39, 41

pack ice, 31, 41, 43, 74
pancake ice, 34
pardon, 63, 74
penguins, 46
Perfect Storm, 18, *19*
permafrost, 46
pirate, 61–72, 74
polar bears, 41, 43, *44*, 45
polar bears, 46
Pollard, George, 49–55
prey, 49, 74
privateer, 63–64, 74

rogue wave, 5–6, 71
Ross Ice Shelf, 27
Royal Navy, 57, 66
Royal Tar, 56–57

salt in seawater, 34
sea level, 46, 74
sea turtles, 49, 51, 53–54
seals, 43, 45, 46
Shackleton, Ernest, 41–43
shipping, 74. *See also* cargo; whaling

shipping lane, 25, 67, 72, 74
Smith, Joy, 5–7
South Georgia Island, 43
South Pole, 39, 41
species, 36, 74
Spotswood, Alexander, 65
storm surge, 13
storm waves, 71
submarine, 58–59

Talley, Jeannine, 5–7
Teach, Edward. *See* Blackbeard
terrorists, 70–71, 74
Titanic, *24*, 25
tornado, 9, *20*, 21, 23, 46, 74
torpedo, 59
Trans-Continental Expedition to
    Antarctica, 41
tropical depression, 11, 74
tropical storm, 11
trosphere, 7
typhoon, 16

U.S. Coast Guard, 71, 72

Vietnam boat people, 68, 69, 70

water rats, 70
waterspout, 21, *22*, 23, 74
Weddell Sea, 41
whalemen, 31, *35*, 36, 49, *50*, *52*,
    74
whaler, 31, 36, 49, 74
whaling, 31–39, 49, 74

Xhosa tribesmen, 57

yankee, 31–33, 74

About the Author

Award-winning author Carole Garbuny Vogel loves the ocean and lives 90 minutes from the beach. Her favorite water sport is boogie boarding, which is a lot like surfing but instead of standing up on the board, she lies flat. On beach days when the waves are small, Carole enjoys reading a good book or strolling on the sand looking for shells.

On workdays, Carole Vogel can usually be found "chained" to her computer, wrestling with words. She specializes in high-interest nonfiction topics for young people. Among her many books are *Nature's Fury: Eyewitness Reports of Natural Disasters* (winner of the Boston Authors Club Book of the Year Award), *Legends of Landforms: Native American Lore and the Geology of the Land* (an NCSS/CBC Notable Social Studies Trade Book), and *Shock Waves Through Los Angeles: The Northridge Earthquake* (placed on the Children's Literature Choice List). Carole Vogel is the coauthor of *The Great Yellowstone Fire*, which was named one of the 100 Best Children's Books of the Century by *The Boston Parents' Paper*.

Carole Vogel's books have been chosen for many reading lists, including Outstanding Science Trade Books by the NSTA-CBC, Best Children's Books of the Year by the Children's Book Committee at Bank Street College of Education, and the Science Books & Films' Best Books for Junior High and High School.

A native Pennsylvanian, Carole Vogel grew up in Pittsburgh and graduated from Kenyon College in Gambier, Ohio, with a B.A. in biology. She received an M.A.T. in elementary education from the University of Pittsburgh and taught for five years before becoming a science editor and author. She keeps in touch with her readership by giving author presentations in schools and libraries.

Carole and her husband, Mark, live in Lexington, Massachusetts, where they enjoy frequent visits from their two children, who recently graduated from college. You can learn more about Carole Vogel at her Web site: *http://www.recognitionscience.com/cgv/*